GORBACHEV

The Last Leader of the USSR

Written by Véronique Van Driessche
Translated by Jessica Foster

History 50MINUTES.com

MIKHAIL SERGEYEVICH GORBACHEV

KEY INFORMATION

- **Born:** 2 March 1931 in Privolnoye, in Stavropol territory (Russian Soviet Federative Socialist Republic).
- **In office:** 11 March 1985 – 25 December 1991.
- **Major achievements:**
  - the end of the Cold War (1945-1990) and the fall of the Iron Curtain
  - the end of Communist regimes in Eastern Europe
  - the dissolution of the Soviet Union (1990-1991)
  - acceptance of the West and of democracy.

INTRODUCTION

When he was named General Secretary of the Communist Party of the Soviet Union, making him the last effective leader of the USSR, Mikhail Gorbachev knew he would have to make radical changes if he wanted the Soviet Union to get out of the rut it was stuck in. The effects of his actions would, however, be greater and his decisions would have a lasting impact on the history of Russia, Europe, Communism and the Cold War. He was to revolutionise the global order as it had stood since 1945, and the Soviet model that had been in place since 1922.

Although in Russia he remains one of the least popular leaders of the 20th century, the West considers him a hero, and awarded him the Nobel Peace Prize in 1990 for ending the Cold War, after electing him *Time* magazine's Man of the

Year in 1987 and Man of the Decade in 1989. Gorbachev thus brought about a true 'Gorbymania' in the United States. The world can indeed not forget that he strove to make Communism more democratic, that he freed thousands of dissidents, that he granted independence to the Eastern bloc countries, that he brought Russia closer to the West and that he obtained a bilateral reduction in nuclear and chemical weapons, marking the end of the Cold War. His influence on the course of history is therefore undeniable and of extremely high importance.

BIOGRAPHY

Photograph of Gorbachev.

FROM HUMBLE ORIGINS

Mikhail Sergeyevich Gorbachev was born on 2 March 1931 in Privolnoye, a village in Stavropol territory, in the South of the Russian Soviet Federative Socialist Republic, at the foot of the Caucasus Mountains.

Gorbachev came from a family of farmers. His parents, Sergey Andreyevich Gorbachev (1909-1976) and Maria Panteleyevna Gopkalo (1911-1993), worked in a *kolkhoz* (farm in which the methods of production are collectivised). Under Stalin (Soviet leader, 1878-1953), his paternal grand-father had been sent into forced labour in 1934 because he refused the collectivisation of land and was suspected of sabotage, while his maternal grandfather had been arrested and imprisoned in 1937-1938, as he was suspected of being responsible for a secret organisation.

DID YOU KNOW?

Mikhail Gorbachev was born with an angioma, a red mark, on his forehead. This physical characteristic, which did not seem to bother him and which he never tried to hide, made him quite easily recognisable.

A CHILDHOOD SPENT IN THE FIELDS

During German occupation (August 1942-January 1943), the young Mikhail had to work in the fields to feed his village; as his family were desperately short on money, he only started his education again at the beginning of the academic year in 1944. Subsequently, he spent his free time working on farms and, at the age of 17, was awarded the Order of the Red Banner of Labour for his excellent service as a combine harvester driver, which allowed him to consider studying at university. He was a member of Komsomol, the Communist youth division, from the age of 14.

He finished secondary school in 1950, at the age of 19. Until 1955, he studied law in Moscow, at the prestigious Lomonosov Moscow State University (MSU). During this period, he belonged to the student Communist movement, then joined the CPSU (Communist Party of the Soviet Union) in 1952. It was also in Moscow that he met Raisa Titarenko (1932-1999), who was studying philosophy and sociology, and whom he married in 1953 before they finished their studies. Their only child, Irina, was born four years later.

A CAREER OFF TO A GOOD START

Back in his home region, he had a career as an *apparatchik* (a full-time official) in his local section of the Communist Party. Between 1964 and 1967, he studied in the economics faculty of the Stavropol Institute of Agriculture. It was during this time that he met Yuri Andropov (1914-1984), then chairman of the KGB (Soviet intelligence service), who liked him and helped his career progression.

From 1970 to 1978, he was in charge of the Stavropol Regional Committee of the CPSU. In 1971, at the age of 40, he joined the party's Central Committee. In 1978, he was made the Central Committee's secretary of agriculture and went to live in Moscow with his family. On 21 October 1980, when he was only 49 years old, he became a full member of the Politburo (the policy-making institution of the Central Committee of the Soviet Communist Party).

When Leonid Brezhnev (1906-1982) died, he supported the candidacy of his mentor Yuri Andropov for the position of General Secretary of the CPSU and, during his tenure, was responsible for economics and labour. Under the next leader, Konstantin Chernenko (1911-1985), who was already very ill when he came to power, he became the party's second-in-command, deputy to the General Secretary, whom he often replaced at Politburo meetings. As president of the Soviet Union's commission for foreign affairs, he first ventured onto the international scene, shocking his counterparts with his open mind and relaxed nature.

LEADER OF THE USSR

On 11 March 1985, the day after Chernenko's death, Mikhail Gorbachev became the Party's sixth General Secretary. At the age of 54, he represented a new generation of politicians and inspired confidence and hope, two qualities that were necessary given the ruin the Soviet Union had fallen into. He promised a programme of serious reforms and increased acceptance of the West.

In October 1988, he was made Chairman of the Presidium of the Supreme Soviet (the supreme authority of the State). One year later, he organised the first free elections in the USSR. In the same year, he put an end to the Cold War and contributed to the reunification of Germany. In March 1990, he was elected President of the Soviet Union for five years, but the country's economy was in extremely poor shape and nationalism was starting to stir in the Soviet Republics, which were demanding the end of Communist dictatorship. In 1991, following a coup d'état launched by Communist hard-liners (18-21 August), he resigned from his position as General Secretary of the party then, on 25 December, from his position as President of the Soviet Union, which disappeared along with him.

AFTER THE USSR

After the dissolution of the Soviet Union, Gorbachev focused on environmentalism and defending peace. In 1993 he founded Green Cross International, an environmental organisation with the mission of ensuring a sustainable future for all the populations of the world. On 12 March 2012, at the age of 81, he spoke at the opening of the sixth World Water Forum in front of delegates from 140 countries. He said that he was in favour of the creation of an international court, which would "try those responsible for environmental crimes, both business leaders and the heads of state or government" (*News24*, 2012).

He did not, however, turn his back on politics. After standing as a candidate for the presidential election of the Russian Federation in 1996 – in which he received less than 1% of the vote – he founded the Social Democratic Party of Russia, from which he resigned in 2004, then the Independent Democratic Party of Russia in 2008, with billionaire Alexander Lebedev (born in 1959). In 2011, he tried to establish a new Social Democratic Party of Russia, but did not gain authorisation.

Nowadays, he is a fervent critic of the Russian regime led by Vladimir Putin (born in 1952), whose internal authoritarianism he dislikes, but whose role in the Ukrainian crisis he does, however, defend (in 2014-2015, Russia reclaimed possession of Crimea, which belonged to Ukraine).

THE USSR, 79 YEARS OF HISTORY

THE FOUNDING OF THE SOVIET UNION

After the fall of Tsarism (when power passed to the middle classes) and the October Revolution (when power passed to the hands of the Soviets who represented workers and farmers) in 1917, in the context of the First World War (1914-1918) then of a civil war which continued until 1920, the Russian Soviet Federative Socialist Republic (RSFSR), the first Communist State in history, was set up under the leadership of Lenin (1870-1924) and the Bolsheviks, who were renamed the Communist Party in 1918. Their maxim was the leadership of the proletariat (the workforce, according to Marxist doctrine), which involved sharing land between farmers and workers controlling the factories.

The country was governed by the Presidium of the Supreme Soviet, whose president was theoretically the head of state, and the Council of People's Commissars, which made up the government. Behind all of this, the Communist Party, directed by the Central Committee, was in power. The Central Committee's supreme body was Politburo, the political bureau, whose general secretary was the effective head of state.

Lenin addressing Red Army soldiers in 1920.

After imposing 'war communism' (nationalisation of business, banks, industry and even the artisanal sector), Lenin was forced to relax the regime: his New Economic Policy (NEP) in 1921 marked a limited return to market capitalism, which would hopefully boost the Soviet economy.

The Union of Soviet Socialist Republics (USSR) was created on 30 December 1922. This federation of Russia, Ukraine, Belarus and Transcaucasia (including Armenia, Georgia and

Azerbaijan) would group together 15 republics in total.

STALIN'S OMNIPOTENCE

Lenin died in 1924 and the tyrannical Joseph Vissarionovich Jughashvili, better known as Stalin, succeeded him as head of state. Taking advantage of his powerful state police and the bureaucratisation that was becoming widespread, he successfully maintained absolute power for over a quarter of a century, freely imposing a cult of personality.

Stalin and Lenin.

He nationalised all farmland, which he organised into kolkhozes and *sovkhozy*; huge, state-owned farms: this was collectivisation. Those who opposed him were sent to Gulag labour camps, established in 1930. He also nationalised all businesses and, from 1928 onwards, introduced "Five-Year Plans" that assigned each of them precise production targets, which continued to rise for the next five years. This helped the USSR to become the third largest global industrial power, opting for heavy industry (steel, weapons and energy) to the detriment of its population and its consumer goods, and at the cost of significant damage (wasted resources, botched work, etc.).

Between 1934 and 1938, Stalin disposed of all his opponents once and for all, as well as anyone who was unhappy with his regime. This was the period of the Great Purge, also known as the Great Terror, which saw hundreds of thousands of people executed or deported.

THE USSR DURING THE SECOND WORLD WAR

On 23 August 1939, Stalin, who had not managed to secure an alliance with European democracies, signed a non-aggression pact with Adolf Hitler (1889-1945), between Germany and the Soviet Union. On 22 June 1941, however, the *Wehrmacht* (German army) launched a violent attack on Russia, and arrived at the gates of Moscow in the autumn of 1941. But the Russian winter saved the day. In May 1942, the second German offensive and the Battle of Stalingrad, which ended in the first Soviet victory (winter 1942-1943), marked an important turning point in the course of the war, allowing the Red Army to launch a counter-offensive and gain land back from the Germans, until their surrender on 8 May 1945.

Battle of Stalingrad.

At the end of the war, the United States and the Soviet Union, despite being allied against Nazi Germany, found themselves in opposition and created two alliances: NATO (1949), which joined Western democracies (the United States, Canada, Belgium, France, Luxemburg, the Netherlands, the United Kingdom, Denmark, Italy, Norway and Iceland), and the Warsaw Pact (1955), signed by most of the states in the Communist bloc (the USSR, Albania, Romania, Bulgaria, Hungary, Poland, Czechoslovakia and the German Democratic Republic).

THE COLD WAR

For nearly 50 years, the world was divided between these two superpowers and their opposing ideologies, Communism against capitalism. Europe was the main playing field for this rivalry, but it also spread across the rest of the world.

When Stalin died on 5 March 1953, many hoped for a softening of the regime, which seemed to be confirmed in 1956, when his successor, Nikita Khrushchev (1894-1971), condemned the system of repression, the bureaucracy and the cult of personality implemented by the former leader of the USSR: this marked the beginning of de-Stalinisation. The Red Army's crushing the uprising in Budapest in November, however, showed that this softening was only relative. Moreover, the space race and the arms race began in 1957, with the launch of Sputnik, the first artificial satellite, into orbit. This, and the launching of the first man into space, Yuri Gagarin (1934-1968), gave the advantage to the Soviets. In response, the American president John F. Kennedy (1917-1963) launched the lunar programme, under the aegis of the National Aeronautics and Space Administration (NASA).

Construction of the Berlin Wall.

The construction of the Berlin Wall on 13 August of that same year increased tensions between the East and the West, which peaked in October 1962, over the issue of the USSR installing missiles in Cuba and pointing them towards the United States. Nuclear warfare had never been so close to breaking out, and world leaders realised the need to implement disarmament agreements: this was the beginning of a détente.

THE BREZHNEV ERA

In 1964, Leonid Brezhnev replaced Khrushchev, whose results had not been satisfactory, at the head of the Communist Party. The new leader gradually sent the country into a state of stagnation and political immobilism, drowning in bureaucracy and alcoholism. Any dissidence or criticism of socialism was quickly stamped out.

Brezhnev asserted the non-sovereignty of the satellite states of the Communist bloc: this was the Brezhnev Doctrine, which justified crushing the Prague Spring, a liberalisation attempt in Czechoslovakia. Additionally, by programming the deployment of the SS-20 Saber intermediate-range nuclear missiles in Eastern Europe in 1977, then the invasion of Afghanistan by the Red Army to support its Communist regime in 1979, he ended the détente and restarted the arms race.

The West responded by installing the Pershing II American missiles and cruise missiles in Western Europe. In March 1983, Ronald Reagan (1911-2004), elected US President in 1980, launched the "Star Wars" project (or SDI, Strategic Defense Initiative), aimed at creating an inviolable spatial defence system above American territory to protect it from Soviet nuclear weapons. The USSR, which was already spending an enormous portion of its budget on arms, would never be able to keep up.

The economic consequences were indeed catastrophic. The Soviet model had reached its limits in the 1960s and 1970s: growth slowed down, work productivity and capital were stagnating, shortages were increasing and quality of life was extremely low. In addition, the black market, the underground economy and corruption were omnipresent.

At the end of the 1970s, the KGB evaluated the Soviet Union's GNP in terms of added value (value of the quantity produced), according to Western criteria, and no longer just in terms of volume (quantity produced), according to socialist criteria, in order to get a real idea of the economic situation. When they did this, the USSR realised they had been overtaken by Japan and soon would be by West Germany (the FRG), while China, which had begun an economic revolution in 1978 by re-establishing capitalist rules in the market economy, was demonstrating great dynamism. This investigation would be at the root of the reforms implemented by Gorbachev.

On an international level, the situation was not much more promising. The Soviet Union was losing allies, as Communism was less and less appealing, and the Eastern bloc countries were beginning to question the totalitarian regimes and reclaim their freedom. This was notably the case for Poland, in 1979, under the governance of Lech Walesa (born in 1943) and his free trade union *Solidarnosc* ('Solidarity').

ELDERLY LEADERS

The USSR's immobilism under Brezhnev could notably be seen in the lack of replacement of politicians, who remained in their positions indefinitely. At the beginning of the 1980s, all power in the USSR was essentially in the hands of men in their 70s, to the extent that it was described as a gerontocracy.

Brezhnev died on 10 November 1982. Yuri Andropov, the former head of the KGB, succeeded him as the head of the party. Aware of the appalling state the country was in, he started by removing the old members of Brezhnev's team from key positions, and they were accused of incompetence and prosecuted for corruption. He also tried to resume dialogue with the United States. But as he was also an old man, he ended up falling ill and passed away on 9 February 1984.

The next leader, Konstantin Chernenko, who was even older and was already seriously ill when he came to office, died on 10 March 1985. His deputy, Mikhail Gorbachev, a younger man in his 50s, was elected as General Secretary of the Party to replace him.

HIGHLIGHTS

THE NEW WATCHWORDS: *GLASNOST* AND *PERESTROIKA*

On 11 March 1985, Gorbachev was elected General Secretary of the party, while Andrei Gromyko (1909-1989) became the Chairman of the Presidium of the Supreme Soviet. At the age of 54, dynamic and close to the people, Gorbachev represented the new generation of political leaders, formed after the de-Stalinisation of 1956.

He knew that the crisis was not only an economic one, but also a moral and social one, and could only be resolved by completely changing the Soviet system, by modernising and liberalising it. His first reform – a series of measures taken against alcoholism – revealed his desire to awaken the people and involve them more in the political and economic life of the country.

He then launched his imposing project of 'restructuring', *perestroika*, which would respond to economic, social, administrative, institutional and political problems: it was a comprehensive, multifaceted and complex reform. The objective was to democratise the Communist regime while staying true to its founding principles.

As there could be no progress towards democracy without offering the population a certain freedom of expression and information, Gorbachev simultaneously introduced the principle of 'transparency', *glasnost*. Censorship had to be abolished, the press freed, former dissidents rehabilitated, and opposing political organisations and protests authorised. This part of his policies, which was at the origin of the revelation of many secrets, could also be used as a weapon of propaganda against conservatives who might refuse change, arguing that everything was fine, or as an aid in the fight against corruption and privilege, and was proof of good faith for Western sceptics.

POLITICAL LIBERALISATION

From the moment he came to power, Gorbachev announced his desire to restructure the Soviet State and the Communist Party. During his first months, he surrounded himself with a group of reformers who began to place their men within the political mechanism. In 1986 and 1987, he understood that he had to accelerate the democratic process to involve citizens, so that conservative Communists did not block his reforms. He wanted to separate the State mechanism from the Party, ensuring that the latter would keep him as its leader. He thus thought he could safeguard the system by reforming it. He would later have to give up on these reforms.

On 1 October 1988, he was elected President of the Supreme Soviet, succeeding Gromyko. This position was necessary for him to be able to put forward constitutional amendments, and therefore to carry out his political reforms completely legally.

In December of that year, he began his first constitutional reform which, in spring 1989 (26 March-23 May), resulted in the creation of the Congress of People's Deputies, of whom two thirds were voted for in a free election (i.e. by secret ballot and between several candidates) for the first time. This new legislative assembly would be the main body of the Soviet Union's government until 1991. The State mechanism and the Party were thus separated.

In May 1989, a constitutional reform led to the creation of the position of Chairman of the Supreme Soviet of the Soviet Union, which this time was associated with proper functions of a head of state. Gorbachev was elected on 25 May 1989 by the Congress of People's Deputies. He therefore held the positions of both General Secretary of the Party and head of state, which made him the spokesperson for both the Party and for the State mechanism.

During the third Congress of the People's Deputies of the USSR (12-15 March 1990), the role of leader of the Communist Party was officially abolished. During the same congress, the role of President of the Soviet Union was created. Gorbachev was elected to this position for a five-year term.

ECONOMIC LIBERALISATION

Perestroika led to significant changes in the country's economic system, which until then had been entirely planned, centralised and controlled by the State. Gorbachev wanted to liberalise it by gradually introducing a market economy and giving greater autonomy to businesses. He tried to implement a mixed economy in which the State sector, which would remain dominant, would also be relieved in its spending and galvanised by a cooperative private sector in agriculture and services.

The years 1986-1988 saw the adoption of a series of laws and decrees pertaining to state businesses, the functioning of international trade, the reorganisation of the economic administration and the working principles of the markets. These reforms seemed incomplete, however: the main bases of the regime, the leadership of the proletariat and state ownership of the means of production, were not called into question. Gorbachev was the prisoner of a conservatism that prevented him from completely detaching himself from Communism and taking the great step that some of his colleagues advised him to take. He struggled to accept that the role of the State in the economy, the role of the central administrations and the price system might have to change. Additionally, his reforms were met with resistance from the nomenclature, the privileged few of the Communist regime, who wanted to keep their privileges at any cost.

After the promising results of 1986, the situation worsened two years later. The faults in the system's way of functioning had not disappeared, businesses were struggling to be independent, the cooperative private sector encountered significant difficulties in their provisions, the quality of their products was always mediocre, and agricultural under-productivity persisted, as did the shortage of consumer goods.

Social discontentment was soon expressed through strikes, which were now authorised by *glasnost*. Gorbachev was reproached for destroying the centralised planning system and failing to replace it with proper market mechanisms (he did not decide to free prices), making this an unsustainable transitional situation.

WITHDRAWAL FROM FORMER USSR SATELLITE STATES

At the funeral of his predecessor, Chernenko, in 1985, Gorbachev announced that the USSR intended to respect the principles of equality of the States, who from then on would be responsible for the functioning of their own institutions: this marked the end of the Brezhnev Doctrine which prescribed the non-sovereignty of the satellite states. In 1987, on a visit to Czechoslovakia, he reiterated this declaration, and did the same a year later at a UN meeting. His audience remained sceptical, however, until the fall of the Berlin Wall, a symbol of Communist Germany, on the night of 9 November 1989. The lack of reaction from the Soviet leader triggered revolutions before the end of the year across all of Eastern Europe, where democratic movements won out over Communism.

WITHDRAWAL FROM THE COLD WAR AND INTERNATIONAL CONFLICTS

The USSR absolutely had to reduce its weapons spending, as it was slowing down its modernisation. To do this, it had to unburden itself of its costly rivalry with the United

States. As well as attending the Commission on Security and Cooperation in Europe (CSCE) to normalise his relations with Europe, Gorbachev began a series of summit meetings in 1985 with his American counterpart, in order to negotiate the disarmament of the two blocs.

It was not until the meeting in December 1987 in Washington that a first agreement was drawn up with Ronald Reagan on eliminating short- and intermediate-range ground weapons, the 'euromissiles': this was the Intermediate-Range Nuclear Forces (INF) Treaty.

During the meeting that took place from 29 May to 1 June 1988 in Moscow, Gorbachev signed technical agreements on missile testing and atomic experiments with George Bush Sr., who was elected president that same year. In Malta, at the beginning of 1989, the two heads of state declared that they were no longer enemies, thus ending 45 years of the Cold War. The situation between the two major powers continued to improve, and a new agreement was signed in May-June 1990 in Washington, this time related to the reduction and destruction of chemical weapons. One year later, Gorbachev and Bush signed the START treaty (Strategic Arms Reduction Treaty), which envisaged a 30% reduction in their strategic nuclear weaponry.

In parallel with these agreements, Gorbachev withdrew the USSR from all the conflicts linked to the Cold War and to the expansion of Communism. He thus planned the gradual retreat of the Red Army from Afghanistan (completed in February 1989), encouraged the Vietnamese to leave Cambodia (April 1989) and the Cubans to withdraw from Angola (August 1988), and stopped supporting the Communist regimes in Cuba, Nicaragua and Ethiopia. He also normalised his relations with Beijing (May 1989) and resumed diplomatic relations with Israel (September 1990). Finally, he condemned the invasion of Kuwait by Iraq, formerly an ally of the USSR, and supported the United States in the Gulf War (August 1990-February 1991).

Between 1989 and 1991, Communist regimes fell in Eastern Europe and in 1991, several countries announced that they were leaving the Warsaw Pact, which was dissolved on 1 July. Only NATO remained; it was the end of the bipolar world.

THE RISE OF NATIONALISM AND THE END OF THE SOVIET UNION

In 1990, Gorbachev had to face a new phenomenon that developed quickly, stirred up by the principles of liberalisation which he himself had implemented: the emergence of nationalism. From 1988 onwards, the Soviet republics, until now forced into silence and submission, demonstrated autonomist and separatist tendencies, starting with the Baltic republics (Estonia, Latvia and Lithuania), which had never accepted their forced integration into the USSR in 1944. Lithuania declared itself independent on 11 March 1990, closely followed by its neighbours. On 23 August 1989, a human chain was made between Tallinn, Riga and Vilnius, the capitals of the three Baltic countries, in order to request their independence.

At the end of 1990, Gorbachev, abandoned by the democrats, turned towards the hard-line Communists, established a new government and briefly made the regime stricter, leaving the Soviet army to harshly suppress the separatist protests in Latvia and Lithuania. Faced with the reactions of the international community and of Soviet reformists, he returned to a more democratic position. After organising a referendum on 17 March 1991 on the future of the Soviet Union in a treaty that would respect the national aspirations of the republics, he prepared the constitution of a new union of sovereign states. The project was published at the end of July and planned to be signed on 20 August.

In the meantime, on 12 June 1991, the democrat Boris Yeltsin

(1931-2007), Gorbachev's opponent, was elected President of Russia, the largest Soviet republic, whose independence he proclaimed immediately. Moscow became the seat of two rival powers, Gorbachev's USSR and Yeltsin's Russia.

THE PUTSCH OF 1991

On 15 July 1991, Gorbachev attended the G7 summit in London, where he announced his intention to move to a market economy. He put this plan into action on 25 and 26 July during the plenary session of the Central Committee of the CPSU, with the adoption of the "Socialism, democracy and progress" programme.

This new blow to Communism incited the hard-line members of the government, supported by the KGB and the army, to attempt a coup d'état. On 18 August 1991, the day before the signature of the treaty on the new union, they held Gorbachev in his residence in Crimea, stated that he was unfit to govern, declared a state of emergency and occupied Moscow with the army (500 tanks were deployed to strategic points in the town). The Russian president Yeltsin opposed the putschists and the people, who had developed a taste for freedom, supported him, increasing the number of protests. After three days, most of the troops sent to Moscow came round to the side of the resistance and the putschists were arrested. Gorbachev returned to Moscow, but soon had to accept the reality that he no longer had power. On 23 August, Yeltsin suspended the activities of the CPSU in Russia, then across the territory of the USSR; the following day, Gorbachev resigned from his position as General Secretary of the Party and the Supreme Soviet was dissolved. The Communist Party, the glue holding the USSR together, had ceased to exist. In the days that followed, eight Soviet republics (Turkmenistan, Ukraine, Belarus, Moldova, Kazakhstan, Azerbaijan, Uzbekistan and Kyrgyzstan) declared their independence.

Refusing to sign Gorbachev's treaty on the Soviet Union, which they declared to have dissolved, the leaders of the three founding countries of the USSR (Belarus, Ukraine and Russia) decided, on 8 December, to create a Commonwealth of Independent States (CIS), which the other republics (apart from Georgia and the Baltic countries) joined a few days later.

Yeltsin proclaimed that all the Soviet institutions would cease to function at the end of the year. On 25 December 1991 at 7pm, Gorbachev announced in a television interview that he was resigning from his position as President of the Soviet Union. He sent Yeltsin the nuclear access codes, symbols of presidential power: this was the end of the Soviet Union.

IMPACT

FROM THE USSR TO RUSSIA

The Soviet Union no longer exists. The Russian Federation, which is the most significant portion of the former USSR in terms of territory, population and economy, and which is still the largest country in the world, took its place, taking over its position in the international community and inheriting its external debt.

The Russian 'big brother' made a particular effort to keep a stranglehold on the former Soviet republics, which had become new independent states, constituted the nearest foreign countries, and were largely economically dependent on Moscow. The new post-Soviet states, however, wanted greater freedom and there are regularly nationalist reactions towards Russia (the Revolution of Roses in Georgia in 2003, the Orange Revolution in Ukraine in 2004, the Tulip Revolution in Kyrgyzstan in 2005, etc.).

FROM A PLANNED ECONOMY TO A MARKET ECONOMY

In 1992, the decision was made to apply a sort of shock therapy to the Russian economic system, which moved without a proper transition to capitalism (privatisation of businesses) and a market economy (freeing of prices and external trade). This radical change caused widespread chaos (prices exploded, unemployment was rife, GDP halved), leading to a massive economic collapse, which resulted in a major financial crisis in 1998. A significant proportion of the population found themselves unemployed and living in abject poverty, while a handful of well-placed individuals, the oligarchs, became outrageously rich, often though dishonest means.

After the decline of the 1990s, Russia got back on the track towards growth thanks to economic and social reforms, but in particular thanks to the increasing cost of fuel (Russia has a rich supply of oil and natural gas).

FROM COMMUNISM TO DEMOCRACY?

In December 1993, under the presidency of Boris Yeltsin, the Constitution of the Russian Federation was adopted. It regulated the sharing of authority between the president, the government and the parliament (the Duma), giving the appearance of a democratic regime, but with more and more power being accorded to the president. The Yeltsin years were years of economic and social chaos, which put the Russians off democracy and made them nostalgic for a time when work, education and healthcare were ensured by the state.

In 2000, Vladimir Putin, formerly of the KGB, president of the Russian Federation until 2008, re-elected in 2012, wanted to reinstate a strong State. He increased his presidential power by reinforcing the role of the administration and by relying on the army, the police and the intelligence services. He promoted a nationalist ideology and the return of the tsars to Russia, which justified his expansionist ideas. He implemented electoral authoritarianism (no honest competition between the authority in power and the opposition), and reduced freedom of speech, of the press and of NGOS. Hopes for democracy were distant and a semi-authoritarian power developed.

FROM A BIPOLAR WORLD TO A UNIPOLAR OR MULTIPOLAR WORLD?

Following the dissolution of the Soviet Empire, a "new world order" – in the words of George Bush Sr. in a speech to Congress in 1990 – was now in place, dominated by the United States which, as the only major global power, considered it their duty to spread their model of liberal democracy and to monitor adherence to peace and to international laws, acting as the world's law enforcement agency. While the clash between East and West was now over, the risks of war had still not disappeared, as the Gulf War, the break-up of Yugoslavia (1991-1995) and, from 2001, the appearance of terrorism, a new kind of conflict, demonstrated.

After initially making an effort to maintain dialogue and cooperation with their allies while respecting the authority of the UN, the US has gradually turned towards an increasingly individualist politics and a unilateral management of international conflicts. But, while they remain mostly dominant in terms of military power, their global standing, which determines their ability to influence and persuade the rest of the world (which is what we call 'soft power'), is overall in decline. The American model must now compete with the models put forward by emerging powers such as Japan, India, China and the European Union.

SUMMARY

1922
30th Dec.: Founding of the USSR

1931
2nd Mar.: Birth of Gorbachev

1945
Start of the Cold War

1952
Gorbachev joins the CPSU

1970-1978
Gorbachev is director of the CPSU's Regional Committee in Stavropol

1978
Gorbachev is made secretary of the Central Committee

1980
21st Oct.: Gorbachev becomes a permanent member of Politburo

1985
***11st Mar.:* Gorbachev becomes the Party's sixth General Secretary**

1988
Oct.: Gorbachev is made Chairman of the Presidium of the Supreme Soviet

1989
End of the Cold War

1990
Gorbachev receives the Nobel Peace Prize
***Mar.:* Gorbachev is elected President of the Soviet Union**

1991
Gorbachev resigns from his position as General Secretary of the Party
***25th Dec.:* Gorbachev resigns from his position as President of the USSR Dissolution of the Soviet Union**

- Mikhail Gorbachev was born in 1931, in a USSR that was completely under the power of its leader Joseph Stalin, who had imposed authoritarian Communism after the mass nationalisation of farms (collectivisation) and businesses, to which he assigned rigorous production objectives (planning). The USSR quickly became one of the greatest global industrial powers and built a veritable empire after the Second World War, competing with the United States during the Cold War. This apparent success hid a great deal of abject poverty and dysfunction, which would only worsen and lead the country to its downfall.
- Until 1955, Gorbachev studied law and agronomy. He began his career as an apparatchik and rapidly rose through the ranks of the Communist Party, firstly in his home region, then in Moscow.
- In 1985, at the age of only 54, he became the sixth leader of the USSR. The task awaiting him was a considerable one, as the Soviet Union was on the brink of economic collapse. He knew that it would not be able to survive without significant reforms, both political and economic, which would allow it to be more open to the world. He instated *perestroika* ('restructuring' which led to a certain amount of decentralisation) and *glasnost* ('transparency', which granted freedom of expression), in the aim of democratising the Communist system. Additionally, he withdrew from all the conflicts linked to the Cold War and the expansion of Communism, in order to reduce the country's excessive military spending. This was not enough: the economic situation worsened and the Soviet republics, liberated by *glasnost*, began to demand their independence.

- During the summer of 1991, hard-line Communists close to the government attempted a coup d'état, which failed after three days, but left Gorbachev with no authority in the face of the new leader of Russia, a former Soviet republic, Boris Yeltsin, who decided to suspend the Communist Party's activities, leading to the dismantling of the Soviet Union. Gorbachev resigned from his position as head of state on 25 December 1991.
- Gorbachev was awarded the Nobel Peace Prize in 1990 for ending the Cold War and then dedicated his time to defending world peace and environmentalism (by founding Green Cross International).
- His attempts to return to political life in his country have failed, and he remains the least popular 20th-century leader among Russians. However, he is still listened to and respected in the rest of the world.

FIND OUT MORE

BIBLIOGRAPHY

* Bergeron, G. (1992) *Finie, la guerre froide?*. Sillery (Québec): Septentrion.
* Désert, M. (no date) Gorbatchev Mikhaïl (1931-). *Encyclopédie Universalis*. [Online]. [Accessed 22 February 2015]. Available from: <http://www.universalis.fr/encyclopedie/mikhail-gorbatchev/>
* Favarel-Garrigues, G. and Rousselet, K. (2010) *La Russie contemporaine*. Paris: Librairie Arthème Fayard.
* Gorbachev, M. (1987) *Perestroika: New Thinking for Our Country and the World*. New York: HarperCollins.
* Gorbachev, M. (1991) *The August Coup: The Truth and the Lessons*. New York: HarperCollins.
* Gorbachev, M. (1997) *Memoirs*. New York: Bantam Books.
* Gorbachev, M. (2006) *Manifesto for the Earth*. East Sussex: Clairview Books.
* Gorbachev, M. and Ikeda, D. (2005) *Moral lessons of the Twentieth Century*. London: I.B. Tauris.
* Grachev, A. (2008) *Gorbachev's Gamble: Soviet Foreign Policy and the End of the Cold War*. Cambridge: Polity Press.
* Heyraud, H. (1992) *La fin de la guerre froide: perspectives*. Lyon: Presses universitaires de Lyon.
* Lecomte, B. (2014) *Gorbatchev*. Paris: Perrin.
* Mercier, A. and Valo, M. (2012) Gorbatchev plaide pour un tribunal écologique mondial. *Le Monde*. [Online]. [Accessed 21 December 2016]. Available from:

<http://www.lemonde.fr/planete/article/2012/03/13/
il-faut-un-tribunal-international-pour-ju-
ger-les-crimes-ecologiques_1666918_3244.html>
- Perchoc, P. (no date) Gorbatchev et la *perestroïka* :
des objectifs initiaux aux conséquences inattendues.
Nouvelle Europe. [Online]. [Accessed 9 March 2015].
Available from: <http://www.nouvelle-europe.
eu/gorbatchev-et-la-perestroika-des-objectifs-ini-
tiaux-aux-consequences-inattendues>
- Pryce-Jones, D. (1995) *The War That Never Was: Fall of
the Soviet Empire, 1985-1991.* London: Weidenfeld &
Nicolson.
- Rey, M., Blum, A., Wild, G. and Tinguy, A. (2005) *Les
Russes. De Gorbatchev à Poutine.* Paris: Armand Colin.
- Vaïsse, M. (2002) *Les relation internationales depuis 1945.*
Paris: Armand Colin.
- Wert, N. (2013) *Histoire de l'Union soviétique de
Khrouchtchev à Gorbatchev, 1953-1955.* Paris: PUF.

ICONOGRAPHIC SOURCES

- Gorbachev photograph. Royalty-free reproduction
picture.
- Lenin addressing Red Army soldiers in 1920.
© Goldshtein G.
- Stalin and Lenin. Royalty-free reproduction picture.
- Battle of Stalingrad. Royalty-free reproduction picture.
- Construction of the Berlin Wall. © The Central
Intelligence Agency.

FILMS AND DOCUMENTARIES

- *Gorbachev: The Great Dissident*. (2011) [Documentary]. Ewa Ewart. Dir. United Kingdom: British Broadcasting Corporation.

IMPROVE YOUR GENERAL KNOWLEDGE

IN A BLINK OF AN EYE !

www.50minutes.com